GONE FOR THE GOLD: BE RIGHT BACK

10 SELF-EVIDENT TRUTHS

TO SET YOU FREE IN LIFE

By

Cheryl Leone

WITH INSIGHT & WISDOM FROM

David W. Favor

All Rights Reserved.
Copyright © 2007-2014 by Catalyst Group, Inc.
Published by Mighty Fine Books, a division of Catalyst Group, Inc.

Catalyst Group, Inc.
Post Office Box 97067
Raleigh, North Carolina 27624
Telephone: 1-800-892-0283
www.catalystgroupinc.com
Email: lawfirmcoach@catalystgroupinc.com

No part of this book can be reproduced in any form or by electronic or mechanical means including information storage and retrieval systems, without the express written permission of the author. The only exception is by a reviewer who may quote short excerpts in a review.

Contents

GONE FOR THE GOLD: BE RIGHT BACK	1
SELF-EVIDENT TRUTHS	17
TRUTH # 1: THERE IS ALWAYS MORE	18
TRUTH # 2: DREAM! DREAM! DREAM!	22
TRUTH # 3: KNOW THYSELF AND KNOW OTHERS	26
TRUTH # 4: KNOW YOUR PERSONAL MANIFESTO	32
TRUTH # 5: YOU MUST HAVE A "PWAN"	36
TRUTH # 6: DO OR DIE!	40
TRUTH # 7: DON'T BE A CLIFF HANGERS	45
TRUTH # 8: BE BEST IN SHOW	50
TRUTH #9: THERE IS ALWAYS A BOTTOM LINE	53
TRUTH # 10: LIFE IS NOT PERFECT BUT IT CAN BE JOYFUL	56
THE FINAL THOUGHT	58
Dave's Wisdom and Final Thoughts:	60
OUR MANIFESTO	62

DISCLAIMER

This book is designed to provide information in regard to the subject matter covered. It is sold with the understanding that the publisher and author are not engaged in rendering legal, counseling or professional services. If legal or other expert assistance is required, the services of a competent professional should be sought.

Every effort has been made to make this book as complete and as accurate as possible. This text should be used as a general guide and not as the ultimate source of written information.

The purpose of this book is to educate and entertain. The author and publisher shall have neither liability nor responsibility to any person or entity with respect to any loss or damage caused, or alleged to be caused, directly or indirectly by the information contained in this book.

DEDICATION

There are two special people that get to hear this publically, and it's long overdue.

To Angel Carey, sister of my life and Dave's heart, who has read everything we have written ten times and has refused to take no for an answer when we try to quit. She has walked this journey with us and has made it so much easier. This book seems written about her and her journey, but perhaps she will write her own book. When you get someone like an Angel in your life, be joyful.

To Michelle Joyce, our niece, who has made us recognize the talent that runs in this family and the willingness to believe we truly are in the summer of our lives. She has made us understand there is much more to being an Aunt & Uncle, and she has allowed us to share her life with her insistence since there seems to be great value in having an Aunt Cheryl & Uncle Dave.

Finally, we can't forget Connor, our great nephew, who shared with us his special powers that I am sure made this book become what it is.

APOLOGIES

I write like I talk and how I mentor. If I intermix I and we, it is because Dave and I are so intermixed. I have done my best to have this edited and re-edited, but at some point you just go for it. That is what I have done. Writing should be like love. You should never have to say you are sorry, but just in case...if any edits or grammar are missed, I am sorry.

Dave probably thinks the same way. I have asked him to provide his usual insight and wisdom to the book. Any comment by Dave is his own, without me changing one word. For a change, he gets to talk, and we need to listen.

WE WANT TO WIN THE GAME - WE NEED TO KNOW THE RULES

We all want to be champions at something. I have neither the will-power, nor the zest to be an athlete that can make it to the Olympics. If they had an event that chalked up how many books you can sit and read in a lifetime, I would walk away with more Gold Medals than anyone else combined every four years.

Yet each of us has an opportunity to be an Olympian at life, and training is easy. It is based in reality, and it can only get better the more you practice. It doesn't require physical strength or even great mental power. It only requires reasonable endurance and a willingness to see life as it is, not what we are told.

I admit I didn't see this for the majority of my life and one day I had a wake-up call. Believe me, all of us have them. The question is whether or not we listen. Sometimes you only get one.

I absolutely 100% believe there are three types of people in this world. Imagine you are at the highest cliff in the Grand Canyon. You look miles down and there are scraggy cliffs, rushing rivers, and a 100% probability factor you will die if you go over the edge.

The first person runs to the edge of the cliff, looks down, and says "never going to happen, I don't want to die." The second person runs to the edge of the cliff, looks down and says "I can do this, but I need a parachute and some training." The third person runs to the edge of the cliff, never slows down, and yells, "what the heck" and jumps figuring he or she can learn to fly on the way down.

Which are you? For the record, unfortunately or fortunately, I am the third one. This book is for all of you that need to be the second one.

This is about leaping off the cliff and landing in such a way you achieve your heart's dream. It is about finding peace. It is about finding joy. It is about fun and it is about feeling your life's purpose on purpose.

Why listen to me? An expert is someone who has a high degree of skill or knowledge on a certain subject. If that is true, then I am the expert of all times on living. I see myself as this ageless woman who took a life-time to get some things right. I am still not there, and I may never fully understand. Every wrinkle (obviously smile ones) I earned. I have endured more than most and not as much as others. I try my hardest to do what is right and sometimes I win and sometimes I don't. Each try is what is important and I am an expert in trying.

I tell anyone who asks for help this. I may be right, or I may be wrong. I am not going to tell you what to do. What I am going to tell you is what I did or what I would do based on my experience. I am going to tell you the truth from my perspective. What you do with all of this is your choice.

A mentor works very hard for a trusted relationship. I hope that is where my expertise comes.

THE PARACHUTE

Unless you are Superman or Superwoman, you need a parachute if you are going to leap off tall buildings in a single bound. You already have a parachute. You just don't know it. I am just like you. I have my ups and our downs. I have the best dysfunctional family anyone could desire (bless you all). I worry. I dream. I have made more than my fair share of mistakes and will probably make many more as I stay in this journey called Life.

I have this band of people that have come together and bonded with me by choice or by accident or brought together by some higher power for a purpose I don't understand. Never the less, we are a bonded clan; slipping and sliding through this life creating memories together; cheering our success and understanding our failures; sharing each other's dreams; creating loving bonds; sometimes hurting but more hugging and kissing to make it better; living, loving and laughing; defending and protecting; and weaving these fragile threads into a strong chain that cannot be broken; a circle of life forms we call 'our family'.

Dave and I are the traditionalist generation, but there is nothing traditional about us. Whether by design or some catalytic event, we can't understand, Dave and I have been blessed with the most unusual collection of people called family you might ever know.

I don't think either of us recognized how valuable family was when we were growing up. We didn't have an appreciation of family dynamics. It was only when we grew up and grew older that we realized how much 'our family' is such an integral part of our lives. They are the guide ropes on our parachute that allow us to land gently on any rocky shore.

Each of us has two children with spouses and three grandchildren we share between us. These kids and grandkids are truly A-okay. They allow us to live our life as we desire, and they trust us to always be there when they need us. They generously allow us into our lives and let us give lots of advice, most probably not needed. They aren't perfect, and for that I am grateful. If there were to be a do-over, it might be raising children. I learned on the job so to speak and didn't have the resources that today's parents do. Yet amazingly these children of ours are right on track for where they want to be (not my dreams, theirs). We try to give them room and yet we feel the need to have them in our room. We struggle to find the right balance with our children.   Love and gratitude are so understated for what we feel about Beth & Shawn & Parker, Scott & Lisa, Wendy & Chuck & Daniel, Tony, and Jason & Stacy.

When we didn't think life could get any better along came Glen & Sue Noble, who knew how much we needed friendship as well as "familyship". They came to us as in-laws for our daughter and stayed and became our friends. Heck we even got them to move here. We not only have their son but also their daughter,

Robin, and her partner, Amanda, and their two gorgeous children, Rowan and Reese, who are now in our lives.

Don't think our circle can get bigger? In 2013 Tony found his biological family. They are wonderful and now have joined the band. His Mom, Jan, had regretfully died before Tony found her. Yet in her obituary she listed him as a son. What an amazing gift! Because of this, now we have a bigger family circle who have jumped in and care for us as we care for them. We have Sarah & Ivory with Jason, and Christine, Rob, Zack and CJ. With them came Aunts Mary and Terry and all of theirs, and I am sure there is more family out there.

I'm not through. You have to count the granddogs and grandcat. So count in Atticus, Piper, Scout, Bea, Gracie Cat, Sydney, Jake and our beloved Sheltie, Mr. Bojangles. Enough! Probably not. We have Savannah, Hearsay, and Buckeye and Mr. Bill waiting for us at Rainbow Bridge. God how animals provide you that sense of completeness.

Both Dave and I lost our parents far too soon and before we understood aging. There are no do-overs, and we want the younger generation to know this. The values of our parents guide us. We see it in our value system and the virtues we keep expanding. We are trying desperately to pass these on to those that will follow in our footsteps, and they do. We call them shared values. Our parents would be proud we think.

We each have two incredibly zany sisters which make for a fantastic four (Harriett, Barbara, Angel and Charlene) and they give us Ully and Dean (with Bill having left us far too early).

Being Aunt Cheryl is my favorite role outside of immediate family because I can be the family Auntie Mame. Our siblings have given us such great nieces and nephew. Add to that the whole group of Jerry's family in Pennsylvania that let me keep my Aunt Cheryl hat after the separation. That makes me shake my head sometimes, but there they are and here I am. Dave loves being an 'Uncle Dave'. You only have to see his face light up when someone like Connor shares his magical powers with him. Some we see or talk with lots and some only once in awhile but don't doubt the love and respect that exists between us and all of them.

I can tell you this. Dave and I each had long-term relationships with former spouses (his with Carol and I with Jerry). What did and didn't work is irrelevant. What is relevant is that we kept both in our lives? When Carol grew sick, we gladly and willingly took that journey with her. We remained with her for over three years until she left us far too soon. And as to Jerry, all three of us have a respect for each other and the time we share and share now.. We wish each other well. We don't forget the roots we started. Neither of us could throw away the many years we had with Carol and Jerry. There were good times that need remembering. We have children that need to know that. It is simply right for us.

The threads of this tapestry we call Family is going to make a beautiful cover one day for our lives. They are indeed the wind beneath our wings.

Only you can decide what kind of parachute you need. Both Dave and I agree for us it is our band we call family coupled with our values and a few virtues we have learned to develop. We add to it our instincts and our knowledge. We use the self-evident truths we have discovered to complete the fabric. We have a very strong parachute to hold us up as we learn to fly and soar.

Dave and I strongly feel it is our mission and our goal to help others get to where we are. Being a mentor, whether in business or in life, is a position of trust. It is an opportunity to develop relationships that allow us to transfer our knowledge to others. That is our legacy.

You already have your parachute. As you continue reading, you are going to recognize your parachute. You'll soon be able to use it to soar to heights you never dreamed possible.

BEEN THERE, DONE THAT

Dave and I each had a different reason for starting the journey, for taking the road less traveled, and we feel we have exceeded beyond our wildest dreams. We believe there is much more to come. We have survived in spite of all that life has thrown at us. We still believe in a brighter tomorrow and our ability to make a difference and achieve more success for ourselves, our clients, and our friends and family.

We both are serious cancer survivors. We both had long term marriages that did not survive. We have had and do have successful careers, and this was all before we were 60.

We have what some tell us are serious health issues we deal with, but we don't see them as impediments to our life. We each have suffered despair and disappointment. We have almost given up, but with some inward determination, something made us reach out and pull ourselves up.

Despite bumps in the road, every day, we put one foot in front of the other with enthusiasm and passion. To do less is like giving in. We don't give in.

We simply don't see an end in sight; Dave is 72 and I am 70. (I actually tell people I am 82 just so I can hear that blessed gasp of how well I look for my age).

We are just like you. We are worried about the economy, concerned about our retirement accounts, want our children to have a greener tomorrow, and hope we are making decisions that will create a future world of hope and prosperity for our grandchildren, and we are afraid we might not be. Yet, we are still making plans, creating visions, and believe there is more gold out there we can win.

When I was seventeen, I graduated from high school with a scholarship in hand to attend a well-respected journalism school. My dream was to be a foreign correspondent for a national newspaper. Unfortunately due to environment, financing, and generational attitudes, I was unable to accept the scholarship (I was advised by my father that I would just get married and have kids and a man should have it to support his family. Really!) I started working for a judge in a small town in Ohio. At 18, I joined the Marine Corps to travel and see the world (HA! I stayed where I trained at Parris Island, SC). I married a Marine (Semper Fi), had a child and lost him at 3 months. I had daughter, Beth while Jerry was in Vietnam. We adopted Tony when Jerry retired.

Jerry was a career Marine with far too much time in Vietnam. He served all of us with honor and distinction and probably didn't hear it enough from this country. He and I had a thirty year run at marriage. We married while I was way too young. We went our separate ways before we actually did. We stayed because that is what our generation did. Somehow we had been able to keep a friendship going when the marriage didn't survive. I am there for him when and if he needs me. Somehow we have made all of this work as they say, for better or for worse.

After the Marine Corps, I went on to work for law firms holding about every position within a firm. I finally went into management because I kept having these scathingly brilliant ideas about how to make law firms a business. I built my reputation as a visionary and a planner. I taught myself, and I learned from others. I kept taking courses and with technology running full speed I kept myself self-taught and self-learned.

I quit working for others and started my own businesses. I succeeded at some and I failed at others. I kept consulting with law firms because I seemed to understand what made them tick. I was working for a law firm client when I met Dave.

We have been together since 1999. We have had an amazing journey of love, commitment and learning how to live life as it should be lived. He was doing consulting after retirement. Together we formed Catalyst and have been partners in both business and life since.

I find myself at this stage of my life mentoring not only law professionals but also other professionals and small business owners. Lately, that has expanded into self-mastery and leadership mentoring because there seems to be such a need out there.

These past fifty years of business have put me in contact with such incredible people who are struggling to achieve their dreams, and I find myself in awe at how hard they will work to get there.

As Dave and I developed a high performance theory for professional practices and small businesses, we realized there was more to it than just applying best business practices. We also had to help develop best life practices. Our clients were winning the business game but losing the mental game of life. We found that they went hand in hand. It was not only necessary for the owners but also for the employees that worked for them.

We changed to what we call 'The Catalyst Way". We began to make our clients develop a personal life plan of wants, needs and dreams. Once we got that into some manageable form to their satisfaction we helped them design their professional and business plan to support it. All of a sudden it started to make sense. We teach that you can convert in a dream into reality, and we do it, time and time again.

We are neither consultants nor coaches. If you look up the definition of a mentor, it simply says a wise and trusted counselor. Each of us are mentors in business and in life. We have found that our roles as teachers of best business practices and life plans allows us to do what we do best, put out there our knowledge for the taking.

I carry many hats and play many roles for others. They range from the career person to the mother to the aunt to the strong friend to others it seems that my zany look at life, using a great deal of common sense mixed with reality, rings a bell in people. The one I wear the most proudly is that of the partner to Dave with a relationship I always suspected could be had for the taking.

EVERYONE SHOULD HAVE A DAVE

Of all the people I have met in my life or have had the privilege of knowing, none has had more of an impact on me personally and professionally than Dave. He is a highly intelligent, thoughtful, quiet man. He is far too organized and once you meet him you understand why he was a project manager with IBM. He is a thinker who will suddenly come up with a solution that makes you wonder why you didn't think of it because it is simplistic and workable. Our clients (and friends) will tell you that Dave is theory, and I am practical and together it is a winning combination.

I met Dave Favor in 1999 through a business internet connection. He was coming out of a long term marriage, retirement, surviving prostrate surgery of the worst kind. Life had turned upside down for him. I had been on my own some ten years and right where I wanted to be. I had a law firm that wasn't doing that great technology wise and Dave was the expert consultant. I asked him to help and how much would he charge. He asked how much could I pay and I said maybe $35.00 per hour. He said that was fine. Later I learned he made ten times that amount doing the same work. That was my tip off that we would not only be business partners but life partners.

We want to be married in Disney World, but until the government changes their crazy laws on insurance coverage for former military wives we can't because I lose that valuable coverage. Our generation isn't supposed to live together, but the family just laughs at us when we say that. We are fine with what we have.

Dave truly has a heart of gold and a high standard of integrity. His kindness and compassion for others makes me want to be a better person. His insistence on a good value system in his life has made me realize the way life should be. His willingness to let me continue to give him advice (on the same subject many times) shows his ability to put up with almost anything. Together we have learned that life was truly meant to be lived with a great deal of passion, humor, and compassion. We are the senior generation learning how to stay ageless in a fast changing world. We haven't even begun to live life as much as we want, but we make great strides each day. Together for the past thirteen years, Dave and I have shared much laughter and love. He has shown me what true relationships are about, whether it is business or personal.

We have a saying that when Dave talks, we all shut up and listen. (Dave says quietly that he doesn't say much because I don't give him a chance). Dave didn't bargain to get involved in law firms or other professional practices and Catalyst. As I said, he was with IBM over 30 years. Throw into that mix, he was an ISO auditor as well as a former Baldridge examiner, and you get the general idea. He has been a consultant with Fortune 500 companies..

Dave has written a book 'From Planning to Profit' and has his life story somewhere in him. He joins me in this book using his usual candid thought process. We write together for some magazines and professional associations. We speak together on all sorts of topics.

Dave and I practice what we preach and teach. We have a personal manifesto (you will learn about this) and each year on January 1st we update our personal plan (it keeps getting bigger and bigger.

As Dave says, everyone has a trump card. That is what happens when you swear nothing will come ahead of your dreams, but sure enough, someone throws out that trump card that stops you. For us, we are each other's trump card. We work on making sure we come first with each other.

Dave and I go beyond love. We believe we are meant to be. We share a deep respectful relationship that makes us better people. Through the mutual respect and strong bonds we share, we find ourselves walking this path in a way few others do, and it is right for us. You will find the right path for yourself. If you don't have a Dave, there is one for you. Just be willing to change and grow.

At this age, I still see limitless opportunities, and it causes me sorrow when I see people half my age settling for less.

THE CATALYST WAY

I am the company's CEO (Chief Energy Officer). I am the visionary. I believe I can do just about anything. I have more ideas than are reasonable. I am enthusiastic and upbeat. I like people. I thrive on adversity. I think life was meant to be lived with a great deal of zest. I give advice freely, and my greatest kick is when I see it work for other people. I simply do not know how people survive this life without a sense of humor because humor makes the unbearable, bearable.

I am also a sad person sometimes. I tend to jump off cliffs without thinking. I push people too hard. I tend to have unreasonable expectations, and I get frustrated when they aren't met. I should probably spend a few years apologizing for all the stupid things I have done, but instead I try to do good works to make a difference as a way of saying 'sorry'.

Dave is very processed base. He will ponder and think things through and then come up with a solution that has step by step how to get things done. He has to research it, and that intelligence he carries well gets to a point I seldom do..

What turned into a small consulting job for Dave has allowed him to have his life-time dream of building businesses for others and of writing, teaching, and consulting. His balance of his strengths combined with mine gave us an edge. More importantly, this merging of complimentary business styles also gave each of us a second chance at developing and supporting a relationship as adults. This relationship has been more loving and satisfying than either of us ever imagined. We believe that it takes lots of living to understand how to live.

Catalyst Group, Inc. was born in 2001 as a way to provide mentoring to service professionals and businesses. Our work has focused mostly on law firms or lawyers, but we have our fair share of other businesses. We now have expanded Catalyst into a mentoring firm for people wanting to own their own businesses. The economy has opened up this whole big world for these budding entrepreneurs. They need help and deserve it.

We believe you are successful when you are serving others, and we have realized that without defined values, you don't go anywhere. We also know without a doubt that the values in your personal life must match the values in your professional life. "Pick and Choose" philosophy is not an option when it comes to values.

We believe virtues are those signs of moral character that you learn and develop, and you have to pick and choose which ones make you a person of character. You don't get these free of charge when you are born. You learn as a matter of character what your life virtues are.

We teach anyone who will listen that you must create a personal plan for success before you create a professional plan. Your career is simply leverage to get you where you want to be personally in life. This philosophy has lead Catalyst to only work with clients who are willing to implement values based managed practices and businesses. It is indeed a 360 world now. We insist they have action plans. We even plug in accountability, so there is forward motion.

We don't market for clients as word of mouth seems to serve us well. Perhaps someday if we decide we want to be a bigger company we will, but for now we are doing exactly what we think we were meant to do.

We believe we are agents of change and cause many a catalytic event when personal and professional lives are changed for the better. It is built with some very specific boundaries of what and whom we will work with. Those that come into our lives are still here, amazingly in some form or fashion, and we are in theirs. We believe we have made a strong difference with our clients. While we are a for-profit company, we are one that will never achieve that at the expense of ourselves or a client.

We are constantly asked what we do. Dave stumbles and goes into a 10 minute elevator speech. I simply say 'we convert dreams to reality'.

Dave's Wisdom:

When you look at life or business, there is a simple process that we believe that we must complete. First you define your beliefs, than your values, then things you are passionate about, and eventually you determine your purpose. After that, you define your vision. This is the ideal path you want to be on, whether life or your business. The problem is reality. You're on your path and reality hits. We opt for short-term happiness every time. We get off the path. We compromise. We redefine our purpose and vision. We start down another path.

After several of these shifts, we forget what our original vision was. Our need for acceptance pushes us to follow someone else's path. All the self-help books describe an ideal path, not reality. Sometimes we come close but more often we reach a dead-end. The same is true for business or life. We can find "best business practices" and can spend a lot of resources to define a strategic plan. We still fail.

What causes us to, so easily, fall off our path? Part of the explanation is that circumstances are not one-dimensional. Life is complex and filled with unexpected events. The best plan possible cannot be flexible enough to accommodate all that can happen. It's for this reason that, in business or life, strategic planning is essential. That's where you attempt to figure out all the unexplained events that could happen with action plans. Even then we tend to put the plan on the shelf. We deal with events throughout the day and have a tendency to forget all the planning we did.

When you stand back and look at this ambitious picture you will see that our day is filled with events and decisions. I have observed that most of us tend to think and react similarly. What I see is that we tend to always search for happiness. We also want to be right, accepted, and viewed as someone that is in control. We also want to be viewed as someone that contributes positively to any circumstance. Failure is never our intent. With all of this going on with every event, we are not inclined to review our strategic plan. Every day we deal with hundreds of events and decisions.

We can see many examples of this all around us. Look at people trying to diet or stay on a budget. It is easy to fall off the path. Sometimes we get so far off our ideal path that we get lost, and it is just easier to stay on the path we are on or just to stop and restart the whole process again.

So what is the answer? I believe that our ideal path cannot be defined so narrowly that we fall off with no effort. Our purpose should be broadly defined so that there is room for some unplanned events and for some self-correction. The key to doing this is to have a well-defined belief, a good set of a few well-defined values and an intimate understanding of what you are passionate about. Now work on a strategic plan that allows for your natural inclinations to be accommodated as you walk your path. Look at the vision you have created. Does it include those activities that you are passionate about? Does your path violate your beliefs or values?

SELF-EVIDENT TRUTHS

Dave and I constantly marvel over how we got where we are. We have come to the conclusion that what we know and what we do truly is common sense, reality based living. We took this thought and decided there were certain truths that if accepted and worked upon, could get you to live a life of joy, unbalanced though it is. You could achieve your dreams if you had certain truths to guide you. Again all of it is s common sense, reality based living.

Throughout the book, you will see inserts by Dave on his take of what I have said. I told him they would remain unedited by me. We are relying on hands-on experience we have used to make things work. We are telling real stories about real people. That is why we call ourselves a common sense approach couple.

There are many, many books out there that tell you "tricks" to becoming all you can be, how to find the gold, and how to be personally and professionally happy. The gold is yours for the taking. Just don't talk about it. Don't let us find you doing that. Join us and put a mental sign on your door that says you have indeed "Gone for the Gold" and you will be right back for more.

Everyone has a different story, but when you read all the books (as we have and continue to do so) it all boils down to your belief system.

If you believe you are destined for something more than you have right now,

If you believe you haven't reached your pinnacle of success,

If you believe you should be making more money than you do with less effort,

If you believe in yourself and your talents

If you believe you have more to offer this world and yourself

Then, like us, you can have it all. Each journey starts with the first step, and as we all know, the journey is much more important than the destination.

So here we go. If only one thing we say makes a difference, then we are winning, and we hope you find what you are digging for.

TRUTH # 1: THERE IS ALWAYS MORE!

We get involved when people call us because they are unhappy and dissatisfied. Usually, they are at a crossroads in their lives where what they have accomplished seems pointless, but they can see no way to make it change in the future. This can be exhibited by working too hard with little results, no forward motion or extreme unhappiness with their choice of a career or life in general. You answer enough of these calls, and you get pretty good at spotting the trends. We were seeing midlife crises far earlier than ever before.

We watch our family circle, and we see far too many of our family and extended family and friends struggling to make it through life while raising their children in the same environment. There is a sense of hopelessness that they are stuck exactly where they are. We fear this is just an on-going circle with the newest members of our family.

In one of our brain-storming sessions, because of my natural enthusiasm for coming up with one more "scathingly brilliant idea", we started asking ourselves at what point do people start to question "is there more?", and are they likely to change. If they aren't, why not?

A mid-life crisis usually occurred when you realized your life was about half-way over, and you hadn't done what you wanted to do. Guess what? We are living longer and better and instead of mid-life crisis there are what we call belief in life crisis events occurring more than once.

In our opinion, the first crisis is between 30 and 35. College is over with. You have settled into whatever career path you have chosen. You may or may not have found a spouse or partner that may or may not be what you want. Children are there, or you are feeling a sense you are running out of time.

There is dissatisfaction that you have made a wrong decision, and you are stalled. This dissatisfaction will stay with you until something changes or you accept an inevitable life of sameness. You wonder if this is all there is, and your mental mind might say 'yup.'

Whether you change or not, we believe you get a second time around 50 to 60. This is when you recognize the kids are gone; you have had a career and you are trying to figure out how to do the last one-third of your life. You can't see the forest for the trees. Those aches and pains you dismissed in your forties are here to stay.

We believe there is now a third crisis, and it is about our age (beginning 70's). You really accept that you are in the winter months of your life, and you want to make sure you have a legacy in this world. You start to make sure you have filled your famous bucket list, and begin to question your faith in a higher purpose or life after this one.

Each of these belief crises (and there could be others trigged by events) makes you stare your life in the face and make a change. You have to decide if you stay on the same road or do you start a different journey.

We wish we could tell you we see only certain types of people are affected, but we don't. We work with people with or without higher education. We work with people from professionals to small business owners. We have met with so called people of fame, and we drank beer with a truck driver (By the way, the trucker driver seemed a bit more grounded in reality). Everyone at some point questions the path they are travelling. This is a healthy thing. If you don't change in some manner, it is unhealthy.

We are also an instant gratification society; young and old alike. We don't want to plan, build and work for future gratification – we want it all, and we want it now. It has absolutely nothing to do with work ethic (a whole other book we intend to write). It has absolutely everything to do with reward and "THE PAYOFF" while we can enjoy it.

It seems to be common knowledge that today's high school graduate stands a good chance of having a minimum of six to eight careers in his or her lifetime. No more do we start something and work the rest of our lives for the same company, in the same profession, or doing the same thing. We live longer. We are active well beyond yesterday's golden years. We have bigger dreams, and we want far more than our parents' ever dreamed of having. Frankly, human beings get bored, but there is hope.

Being healthy, wealthy and wise is a journey, and we believe with all our hearts that the journey is more important than the destination. If you take the journey with resolve and commitment, with zest and enthusiasm, and with a dedication to making a change, you will succeed beyond your wildest imaginations.

Someone once asked me if I was happy. I had to stop and think since my answer depended on what was going on in my life at any one given time. I believe unhappiness evokes change and through change comes brief moments of happiness because you did something about your life. Then if you are like the majority of us driven dreamers, you will find yourself unhappy (or dissatisfied) again, and the process has to restart.

Thus, I would caution you that neither this book nor any book or author in this world is going to make you "happy". I hope that I make you a little unhappy so you can change because through change comes better things. Even failure brings about a good thing because it makes you keep trying.

Is there more? You can bet your last dollar on it. There "is more" whether you are 30, 40, 50 or even 60 or 100! I have a secret belief medical science will cure death, so why should I not think there is more? Because once you understand the process, understand that success is always fluid and always growing, and understand that true happiness comes from converting dreams into reality then you will always ask the question "Is there more?"

A belief there is more creates change. Change promotes growth. People should not be afraid of change. Rather to be healthy, wealthy and wise, you have to be constantly changing because you will be constantly growing.

Dave's Wisdom:

When I met Cheryl, I had my entire life planned out. I believe in planning and having everything documented and written down. On the other hand, Cheryl on any given day will have some scathingly brilliant idea about what we can do and off we go. While it is a little tough on the nerves, we tended to balance each other. She also taught me that dreams can come true. It took me moving outside of my safe zone, and it was the best thing that ever happened to me. As we get older or more secure in our profession, we tend to think we have the answer, and we get tunnel vision. While we feel safe, we are not growing. Life is not a static business project. You have to take chances to expand your vision. You need confidence to keep yourself going when times get tough. Put yourself in your vision. What are you doing? What are you feeling? Add some passion to the mix.

Life is all about learning, taking chances, forming relationships and being true to your beliefs. Sometimes these things cause conflicts, and you have to learn to balance.

TRUTH # 2: DREAM! DREAM! DREAM!

At this point, if you are over 50, you can now stand up and sing word-for-word the old song by the Everly Brothers, Dream, Dream, Dream. It is the start of all that you can imagine in your life. I guess if you are under 50 you might think about Dream Girls.

Walking through a bookstore one day, I saw a metal bookmark with the following quote by Carl Sandburg, "Nothing happens unless first a dream". This has always been true and will always be true.

Without imagination – without dreams – without the desire to be more tomorrow than you are today, you will be exactly where you are now 50 years down the road.

Children love to dream! They can fantasize about anything they want, but as we grow older, for some reason we lose the magic of dreaming. Nothing is worse than a responsible mature adult. Millionaires dream – responsible mature adults do not.

Without dreams, you simply aren't going to make it. Artificial barriers created by what you believe is being responsible prohibit you from making money, it stops you from realizing your full potential, and it inhibits the very essence of you.

Dreams are free – probably the only thing in life that is. It costs you nothing; it is fun to do, and it opens your mind to possibilities.

We love serious, hard-working clients in their business suits who are made to wiggle their toes in the sand and go back to the basics of dreaming. After all, it doesn't hurt, and frankly it is a break in the routine.

We refuse to do our programs at the client's office. We used to have lovely offices in downtown Raleigh, and we closed them. When we saw clients in our offices, we found it difficult for them to shed the professional ego. If we saw them in their offices, they had to prove to us that they really didn't need to talk to us; that darn ego again. Either meeting seemed to have at the fore-front a price tag of how much will all this cost me.

We then made a drastic decision. We closed our offices. We offered a free half-day consultation at our home, sitting on the back porch in blue jeans, with an agreement to talk, and we would answer any questions they wanted, and we would give them whatever advice we could offer during that time. No Commitment. No expectations. Just two or three human beings trying to find out what was important.

It was a brilliant move if I do say so myself. We started getting people who were truly interested in looking beneath the professional layer. They would come with hat in hand, enjoy our home, playing with our dog, and talk about what they really wanted out of life. We heard stories of failed marriages, workaholic careers, and even worries of ill parents. The career, the office, or the problems became secondary. By removing them from their normal surroundings of day-to-day responsibilities, we got them to remember what it was like before the responsibility of life took over.

We believe one of our best success stories is of a lawyer who came to us with the request to help build a million dollar practice (piece of cake) and ended up doing what was his secret dream; to teach at a small college. He forgot how to dream for himself. We also taught him how to leverage his practice to get him to his dream. Admittedly, he wasn't about money in the long run – it was about personal happiness, of taking the pressure off, and putting the fun back into life. That is okay! Not everyone wants to be a millionaire! Okay, maybe 99% do, but occasionally you get one.

We believe the most common phrase we hear is "but I have responsibilities." Well no kidding! We all have responsibilities. The difference is not to allow the responsibility to be a barrier. When you take care of yourself, you can take care of others

The majority of the people we work with forget their responsibility to themselves, so we have implemented this policy. If you want us badly enough, you have to make a personal commitment to resolve something in your personal life. We have probably been responsible for more weight loss programs than Weight Watchers, but it works. We are teaching our clients that they must take care of themselves to take care of others.

A particularly favorite client of ours came to us with a hopelessness that surprised us. By all respects, he was doing okay. However, he had suffered a couple of career disappointments and had lost control of his office and his life. Upon getting involved, we found out he had a dream to write a book. I asked him to send me some examples of his writing. He did, and I was blown away. He was a writer worthy of reading. Right in the middle of turning his law firm upside down, he committed to writing one small book. He did, and it published very successfully. Although he was surprised, we weren't. It taught him a valuable lesson; don't be afraid to dream, talk about it and do it. It wasn't about being wildly successful with the book but for the joy of writing.

We don't care what you start dreaming but rather that you dream. To define vision, you have to create it in your mind. You have to see yourself as having infinite possibilities. You use words like "when" rather than "if". You become positive rather than negative because you are excited.

There is no right dream and no wrong dream – rather, it is having a dream or maybe two, three or four. Only, it has to be your dream without taking into account any responsibilities or obligations to anyone else.

We surround ourselves with certain people we know see our vision and walk the path with us. We feel as senior management we should set the standard for our clients. At the age of 50 (having lived a half of a century of excellence in our humble opinion), each of us independently made major changes in our careers; leveraged property and assets to support our needs, and started working with a passion for what we do. We do not see us as working but rather having fun. We continue to dream. You would be surprised what we are dreaming about now.

We should not be unique. We should be the norm, and yet we find many people who are stalled in life because they have no vision on how to convert their dreams to reality. If you mention to us that we are getting older, we will glare at you. We are getting better. Tell us we need to slow down and we will just run faster. I hope there are seniors picking up this book who will hear this message: start dreaming again. Age is just a number.

We challenge you to take off your suit, take a walk on the beach, and start dreaming. If you have quit working, then simply start dreaming about what you wish you were doing. Second,

Third and Fourth careers are no big deal. I know a very high level management person who applied to be a greeter at Wal-Mart. Good for him!

There is no limit. There is nothing sacred. There is nothing you can't dream you want to do. Because out of dreams comes a vision. You start to visualize who you really want to be. The vision starts to "feel right". You start seeing possibilities of how to do it. You don't say "if", you say "when". You will find yourself waking up with excitement. The dream starts to take hold. Suddenly, you don't want to stay as you are – you want to be all that you can be.

Here it is. Go dream. It is free, fun and might become addictive. It also might get you to the top of whatever mountain you want to climb.

Dave's Wisdom

For 32 years, I was a proud member of the IBM family. I had it all. Senior Management – world traveler – accolades– and then I retired to start my "golden years". My dad had taught me that a man's worth was based on a well-defined career built on integrity and honesty. I did everything everyone wanted me to, and I had become a success in my own right. And guess what? A required departure physical turned up prostate cancer. I found myself with a premature end to my illustrious life about 20 years far too early. From that day followed surgery, loss of self-esteem, dissolution of my 30-year marriage, and depression. I couldn't see a future for myself. Dreams weren't even part of my vocabulary.

Then, by chance, I met Cheryl, and I took a walk on the beach, I learned to wiggle my toes in the sand, and I started dreaming. I stopped my pity party and suddenly saw hope that I could have a better life. (Basically, I was in therapy at this time, and I was told to get it together and make the most of what I had and could have).

This pearl of wisdom opened me up to consulting with a law practice with Cheryl (I quickly found out that my business logic was not the accepted norm for lawyers). Then we formed Catalyst, and I found out that there wasn't anything I couldn't do if I just wanted to do it bad enough. I woke up each day excited because I was seeing possibilities, not limitations. Do I dream? You bet I do!

People always want to know what you do with a second chance. I can tell you that you dream that you can be anything you want to be. I found enthusiasm rather than despair. I found hope rather than hopelessness. My hidden dream – one I couldn't share because I didn't dare-- was to be a seminar leader and a mentor. I wanted to share my knowledge with others. I wanted financial freedom, and I wanted a strong personal relationship with someone. I have my vision defined, and the path is ahead of me.

All that is great and the right way to start, but every now and then I fall off the path. Distraction is your enemy and will get you off the path faster than anything else. You have to stay focused and true to yourself. There will be a test of course, like my triple bypass heart surgery. That was a bit more than a distraction.

TRUTH # 3: KNOW THYSELF AND KNOW OTHERS

If we concede that everyone can dream the impossible dream, the question then becomes, when does reality set in? This does not mean you have to come back to your perceived "real life", but rather how do you make the dream a reality. A big difference!

We never started making leaps until we realize that any dream built has to have a strong foundation; something that will hold up the rest of the structure. This means you must now define some truths about yourself and the people who surround you.

We believe that there has to be a "people check-up" that makes you sit down and think about the human being body you are living in. We walk people through a process of determining their values, defining their virtues, and building on their strengths and finding support for their weaknesses. It is an honest look at what makes you have the ability to live this unbalanced life with a joy and occasional bouts of happiness.

Out of all the steps, the determination of your true value system is probably the hardest because you must question not only what you believe but what you have lived up until this point. It is not something you treat lightly. Values are non-negotiable. A value will pre-determine every action you take, and when you stray from your value you will not be successful.

What we also teach is that you must surround yourself with people of similar values and virtues. This doesn't mean you all think alike. What it means that the core essence of your being is in alignment with those you count on to help you soar like an eagle. If they aren't, get rid of them in your life. Sounds harsh? Perhaps but it works.

We have found in business relationships, as well as personal relationships, people we know are being held back because they have strong relationships with people who have nothing in common with their belief system. We believe this is why partnerships fail and why marriages fail. True friendships never have this problem.

We had a client who came to us with about the lowest self-esteem we had ever seen. He was an amazing individual; very talented and creative. What we saw very quickly was that he was trying to live a life-style that was incompatible with his belief system. The price of success was killing him. In addition, he was being demeaned on a daily basis by people he called 'my best friends'. We could see it. He couldn't. We are pleased to announce that we worked with him and his practice for over a year and as he grew in control of his life and his practice he started slowly weeding out the nay-sayers and the hanger-ons. He calls us from time to time for a tune-up. He sees himself for who he really is not what others were telling him.

Values are pesky. They can come at you when you least expect it. As you grow your values change and grow with you, hopefully for the better. You learn to let them stabilize you when life becomes more unbalanced than it already is.

There is a big difference between a value and policy. A core value is non-negotiable when it is in play. A policy is something you try to do to the best of your ability. You should have a few core values and perhaps more policies.

Our favorite trick at business seminars is to ask for a showing of hands for all who think honesty is a value. Frankly who in their right mind in front of their peers wouldn't raise their hand! Once all hands are in the air, and believe me we have never had a seminar when they weren't, we ask the attendees how many have told their secretary to tell a client they are not in the office. Amazing how few hands are left in the air.

Thus, honesty is a policy we try to practice, but it is NOT non-negotiable. Sort of like when I ask Dave if I look good in this purple outfit I bought. His answer was brilliant with a simple "of course you do!". If you are totally honest, then you are an idiot. (And for women who read this when a man says "Am I hot or what?" and you don't give the honest answer that question deserves, you just created policy and did not violate a value)

In all fairness, each of us will tell you that defining our values was the hardest thing we did. Before we committed to our lives as life partners, we decided we wanted it different the second time around. We examined each other's values (and virtues) and strengths and weaknesses. We set aside an afternoon. How naïve were we? It took us six months of examining our values, ourselves, and the type of relationship we want during the remaining years of our lives, and we butted heads sometimes. In the end, we made it work

Both of us agreed we were very compassionate people and wanted to help others. However, I would give everything away to help someone while Dave believes only in programs that give people a helping hand up not out. Frankly, we got into some pretty strong discussions about what was compassion. We also got into some pretty good arguments about politics. Once we defined our core values, it was with relief that we found we could live, laugh, and love together. In the end, our core value was the protection of our relationship.

These core values have saved us time and time again. When hardship came, when things happened that caused us to falter, when it seemed that we were headed down the wrong road, we literally stop and step away from the situation and pull out our values statement and make decisions based on those values, and we have won every time.

We zealously guard the dynamics of Catalyst. We have learned the hard way. People who surround themselves with people of similar values are successful. We want clients who have these good core values we do. We aren't special. We aren't better than others. Frankly we think our values are common sense. When you have someone in your life who strays or changes values, there is a clash of cataclysmic (I hate this word because I can't pronounce it 98% of the time) proportion.

We worked with a client who became successful far quicker than may have been normal. He believed and promoted his values based business. We were very proud to have been a part of the set up. He was surrounded by opportunities that increased his wealth. Each time he took another step he always justified why it helped the long term plan. At some point, those decisions became about wealth and self-promotion. People who were with him when he had nothing got left behind when he had something. People who went forward with him had their hidden agendas, but they told him what he wanted to hear. We stepped back because we had a sense of unease. We felt like something wasn't a fit anymore. We weren't unkind. We didn't just quit. He still is going on, and we occasionally talk to him. We wish him well. It doesn't make either of us right. We just realized his path couldn't be ours. Our lives got better.

Dave and I are still here many years later and growing successful in our field because we have kept to the values we have agreed upon; they continue to be the same (perhaps refined a bit) and we won't deviate from them. I frequently say that it is easy to have lofty values when you are successful, but you have to have strong values to keep them when the road gets rocky.

Imagining living and working with people you trust with their core belief or value system. This allows you freedom to do anything. In an atmosphere of trust and respect for the character of people making up your parachute, you know where you stand, and you have explicit trust on how they will act or make decisions.

The best advice we can give is when you find that person or group of people who are not thinking like you or holding true to that inner value, get out fast. This includes people called family.

You absolutely cannot reach your dream if you do not stop and find your core values. You must define yourself now, so you can depend on yourself in the future. When you are clear about your values, you get people to buy into you because they know where they stand with you, and this feeling of security creates trust.

I had a period in my life where I thought I had it all. I made a mistake one time of believing what others said to me about me to make me feel good. I surrounded myself with people who had a different belief system. There was no one big deviation from my values, but just little cracks here and there. Looking back, I probably felt some unease, but it was easy to justify that this is what success was. Suffice it to say the higher you climb the harder you fall. We all make mistakes (in fact it is a requirement to success). I found out the hard way that false friends are with you on the way up, and real friends are with you on the way down – and there are very few real friends. I was devastated, and thought I would never recover.

After recovery, physically and emotionally, I started again, but this time I set my own values in concrete. I have made it my personal quest not to violate my values again, even just a little. I choose carefully what values I have. The ones I have I thought through and committed every bit of my personal being to live and die by them. As a result, my decisions now make me feel free. People know where they stand. I refuse to allow people in my life that do not share the same principles I have and enhance me. I refuse to do business with people who are not of similar values. Thus, my life is filled with people I can trust, and I have a deep loyalty to those people.

I would venture to guess that people who knew me before and who knew me after would tell you they did not see a difference, but I can tell you I felt the difference. If I could have a quest, it would be to tell people – be honest about yourself and your values, and set them in granite. Nothing should make you violate your values. The price is too high, and long-term success will elude you.

Virtues are those things you develop in your life that can be considered part of your moral fiber. They are visible, and a core part of the person you are. Take time to think about what virtues you have. I so believe in virtue of kindness that I will not tolerate unkindness in any form and fashion. Kindness builds. Unkindness destroys. As a result, it is one of the few lines in the sand I put out there and will defend with every breath in me. Start developing virtues that will bring with it success as a human being. It makes a difference.

Finally, know your strengths and weaknesses. Without an understanding of what makes you tick you can't win. No one is perfect, believe me. I like to think I can do anything, but the truth of the matter is there are things that keep me from doing this (math and grammar being a notable example). I build things and people into my world that support my weaknesses and admire my strengths. I think that is what Dave and I have.

Dave's Wisdom:

A lot of your joy will be determined by how you react to the world around you. That reaction will be based on how you interpret events and that decision will be biased by your beliefs and values. Values are going to be the principles that you find mean the most to you. You can't have a hundred values. You would have to hire someone to keep you on your toes. I have learned to pick out those values that seem to say that this is truly what I am about.

If you can understand your values and what they mean, and you are true to them, then you have integrity. People want to develop relationships with those they can trust. Real integrity is doing the hard thing because it is the right thing to do. Don't be so rigid that you will never change. I am always learning.

Finding out who you are means finding out what you stand for. The saying "if you don't stand for something you will fall for anything" holds true. Make sure your values are grounded in reality. Values bleed over from personal to professional from home to business from faith to living. Just make sure it is the real you. Not what you think people want to hear or what you are going to show to the world at large.

One of the toughest lessons I learned was that there is often more than one right answer. That ego thing is tough to control. I loved to be right, but I learned a good value when I let that go. My intent now is to listen to both sides of a story. Not always successful, but it is my intent.

TRUTH # 4: KNOW YOUR PERSONAL MANIFESTO

Believe it or not you are almost there – the foundation is being built! You are dreaming, and you know dreams can come true. You won't accept less than what you have a passion for. Those pesky core values that anchor us are being defined. Those virtues you are developing that define your character are taking shape and more will come. Now you need a manifesto and one that is grounded in reality.

A manifesto is defined as a declaration of one's beliefs, opinions, motives, and intentions. It is simply a document that an organization or person writes that declares what is important to them. You will see our personal manifesto at the end of this book. It is us. It is what we believe. Hold us accountable.

What makes a manifesto so valuable is the fact that it is a constant source of inspiration to you, and one that can often be easily read every day. It is a good way to start your day and get focused. When you're going through something tough, isn't it difficult to keep a steady, objective mind? With a manifesto, it's like you always have access to a calmer, more rational you, and a manifest is public.

We have a white dry erase board in the kitchen to help us avoid senior moments. We try to write one thing each day to make us focus on our personal manifesto. Just a way of saying it is always in front of us.

Try it. Write down your beliefs, motives, and intentions about yourself. A manifesto is an opportunity for you to lay your cards on the table. The question is, what do you really believe? Not a lot of detail but a few high-level thoughts that can be used to guide everything we do.

Until you are willing to make a public declaration of your intentions (your dream), your motives (your values) and your views (vision), you are not committed to the new direction you wish to take. Your personal manifesto is a reminder to you on a daily basis of what your intent is with respect to your life and the way you intend to live it.

Again, the lawyer client who wanted to write the book, made a public declaration of his intent to do so, and he never wavered. I can assure you there were people within his life who didn't give him two hoots for doing it. He also was very public about what type of practice he was going to have and was willing to make any sacrifice to get it to where he wanted. Were people upset? You betcha! However, when people believe you are sincere, and you are taking a stand; they are aware of your intent, and they will know your boundaries. And it happens.

This means you throw yourself out into the arena and say this is who I am, this is what I believe, and this is how I will live, and this is what I want to do! When Dave and I did ours we sent it to all our children. We honestly hope they read it, but we have never asked. We are just saying this is who we are and what we believe. It is what we are doing with our life.

I suspect if you asked people what I am about and what I believe, they would tell you that

I believe in being a positive person 24/7;
I believe kindness wins and will not tolerate unkindness in any shape or form;
I believe you have to give back some of what you take out of this world;
I think humor makes us survive an unsurvivable event; and
I believe relationships nurture our soul.

Once you declare yourself, people buy into you. Those that don't, well my opinion is that they may be the reason you were not living your dream. What naturally follows is peace of mind, a sense of well-being, and an attraction that people are drawn to you. It sounds simple, and that is because it is!

Being true to yourself. Don't say one thing and have a hidden agenda driving you. A hidden agenda is when you say what you think people want to hear to achieve an immediate goal, but underneath you have a second goal that benefits yourself, rather than the greater good.

An example might be that a client tells me it is important that his family come first and that he will change his practice to provide for this but underneath he may genuinely want to have his family come first as soon as he has lots of money. There is nothing wrong with this if that is your true self but be honest about it. If not, people will walk the wrong path with you.

The important thing is to get the cards on the table. If your personal manifesto is to make lots of money and you are willing to sacrifice for it, then say so. I can tell you that people who have hidden agendas (the secondary source of getting what you truly want) just aren't going to make it.

People accept the truth; they don't want hidden agendas. They would rather know up front where you stand. When this happens, and you are comfortable saying how you feel and the direction you are going, you will attract successful people. Successful people recognize this in winners. A shortcut to success is not with hidden agendas or half-truths. It is putting yourself and your dream out there and saying this is who I am and what is important to me. Nothing more and nothing less.

Dave's Wisdom:

After my confrontation with cancer and the start of the recovery process, I learned about meditation. This was all part of my recovery process with a group that had experienced the same confrontation that I had. I would like to point out here that cancer may be scary, but the recovery process after treatment is the pits. Talk about a pity party, I had several of those. Getting back on track, I started reading about having a manifesto, and I started writing one. It is good to know what your personal manifesto is and then put it out there publically. Don't be embarrassed by what you wrote down. Too often we are not being honest. People see what they want to see, and we buy into that. We become what others see not who we really are. This manifesto became a challenge to write down what I really believed in. What happens if people laugh? It turns out that is up to each of us. How we react to life becomes the most important factor. I have learned over the years since I first wrote that manifesto to believe in myself. Of course, I take in all the feedback, and I may even change a few things, but the bottom line is that I have learned to be myself.

If you want to see what is really happening in your life, look at how you spend your time and your money. The first time I did this I got a good shock. I had all kinds of good intentions scheduled on my calendar, but all were canceled. I had all kinds of great projects, but I spent my money on other stuff. Now, I admit that we all have responsibilities and I do not advocate ignoring them. What I do suggest is that you make yourself just as important as all those around you. Spend some time and money on your vision instead of trying to make everyone else successful. One day you wake up and ask, "is that all there is?" So now I put something on the calendar for myself, and I treat it just like any other appointment. Sounds easy, but it isn't. I had a tendency to want to please everyone and put myself in second place. It took a long time to turn that around.

TRUTH # 5: YOU MUST HAVE A "PWAN"

Nothing is more wonderful than Disney's American Tale. As you will recall, the mice wanted to migrate to America based upon the false presumption there were no cats. When they discovered there were cats in America, the lead character jumped up and said "We need a PWAN!" This small saying has become a saying among our family and friends.. Nothing is funnier than to see one of our clients in public say "we need a pwan". I knew our little saying had gained hold when I heard one of his clients say it!

What it means is as you move forward, you must have a pwan or plan! You can't bounce all over the board, but you must have some defined plan of attack. In the business world, this is called strategic planning. In personal living, it is simply The Plan!

The difference between a dreamer and a winner is The Plan! When we originally started out, we were eager to get people to dream. We became so enthusiastic that we opened all sorts of doors for people. We even got them to commit! After all their enthusiasm was now into the do or die stage. Yet every time we came back to the plan we couldn't get our clients to focus and realize its importance.

As we grew in maturity ourselves we realized that it is one thing to be committed, and it is another thing to be committed in writing. Our clients couldn't see the logic of proper planning. We used terms like "strategic planning" and watched the eyes glaze over. We talked about defined time lines, and we watched the eyes glaze over. We used terms like "due diligence" and we watched the eyes glaze over.

Then it hit us. Dreaming, talking, committing are fun things. You get excited energized but preparing a plan is just plain dull work.

We then decided we would prepare the plan for them. Next we found out that our plan kept getting torn apart because it wasn't' exactly what our client had in mind. Again we realized it was putting it down on paper was the problem.

It was simple, our clients were facing reality by making a permanent pen mark on a piece of paper. The moment of truth had arrived.

It was only when we came to this moment of truth for ourselves that we were able to see the problem and realized it was all in the presentation. We had to give our clients something that made sense. Thus, we have learned to explain a plan simply as a roadmap outlining how you are going to get the gold medal. It can be fluid and changing, but at all times it is in place. It is not a strictly held road-map with every crossroad outlined, but rather a broad-based way to make your journey. It keeps you from getting lost but also allows you to wander off the road a bit as long as you are grounded on the basic direction.

Whether you are writing a plan for business or a plan for life, the truth of the matter it is all the same. You start with your current status (where you stand right now). You then put your vision (dream) right out there as the goal. You look at the tools you have right now. Guess what those pesky values are your virtues. You take your manifesto and use it for the guide. Then like a roadmap you start plugging in the miles you need to go each day before you sleep

Like any good trip, the roadmap will have milestones to reach. They will start out maybe a few months apart, then years and heck you may even want to think about decades. The longer out the focus, the less immediate goals you need to achieve there will be, but you have to know your destination to make the journey. The key is to have a plan with good milestones set out so you can see forward motion.

Out of the major plan (which will be revised again and again) come smaller plans. This is true of business planning as well as life planning. Your goal may be to achieve your degree in five years; the sub-plan will be the steps you take for this.

Don't be inhibited by lack of funding, lack of personnel, or inability to get it done. Lay it out as if you have your own dream team behind you. If you need money say so! Once your dream is down on paper it is also less intimidating. The plan should be as if everything will happen as you plan.

To achieve you have to know your obstacles. Doesn't mean you quit. It just means you better know there are cats out there waiting to pounce. Make a list of these obstacles and be honest. The truth faced is the war won.

We can promise you that there are many fine books out there on planning, but it all starts with you. We don't need fancy software. We don't care if it is pretty or written on a paper bag. The trick is to have the plan.

After all, everyone needs a "pwan" to avoid all the cats that are going to be by the roadside waiting for you as you go by.

Dave's wisdom

In the business world, a strategic plan is simply a road-map to help you reach your vision personally or professionally or both. Back in my corporate days I was not a planner. I was the manager that got the plan. Over the years, I learned a lot about plans, and later as a quality auditor I learned what happens without a plan. A good plan has information, objectives, benchmarks, and accountability. Am I an old project manager or what! Oh, benchmark may be another fancy word you don't hear much. A benchmark is nothing more than finding someone else that did the job well and using that plan for comparison. Changing your plan does not mean you have failed or that you had a bad plan it just means that you have learned something new that suggest a better plan. Perhaps you learned something from a benchmark study. Out of strategic planning come all the other plans that will help drive you to success.

I have seen many strategic plans sitting on shelves collecting dust because the thrill of the plan wore off as soon as it was written and delivered to the client. Strategic planning and all its sub-plans are a working, living, breathing road-map of your dream with accountability. In the world of life planning, the same holds true. You can talk and talk and talk but until you commit it to paper and make it a plan it is all talk. There is something about having it down in writing that makes it real.

You will constantly revise it. You will rethink it, but always keeps the changes to your plan in writing. That makes it real and is what you need to succeed.

I have watched our many clients over these years, and it is my opinion that this is the leap they have to make to make it happen. The commitment of time and effort is what makes it work.

Most of the people we have met that are in trouble have no plan. They have never created a vision. They have no idea what they genuinely want. They are reactive all the time. What this means is that they are helping everyone around them achieve their dream but not working on their own. Once you spend a little time deciding what you want to do with your life or your business you can make a plan and make progress. The difference now is that you tend to find others that have related visions and join in. You now get help achieving your plan, while helping others achieve theirs.

TRUTH # 6: DO OR DIE!

Our meetings tend to get ridiculous because we each have such a sense of humor coupled with strong personalities, entrenched opinions, and are all convinced that we know the best way to do something. Thus, it is easy for us to talk something to death. However, we agree on one thing – once we agree we commit, and we throw all our energy into the project, we adopt the "do or die" theory.

We become like the little choo-choo train going up the hill and frequently one or the other start saying "yes we can…yes we can…". Our belief that commitment is the springboard and lack thereof is the death of a dream has propelled us forward even in the face of adversity.

Committed people attract committed people! Surround yourself with people who believe in your commitment with the same zest you do and you will move mountains.

Quit talking it to death! Once you know what you want to do, you have laid the foundation; it is now time to take the leap. You must commit. This doesn't mean that you can't change plans or actions, but you must keep moving forward.

The more forward motion you have, the faster you will go. We believe with the right commitment you can make a million and can change direction in your life; you can stop being a caged buzzard and learn to soar with the eagles.

Commitment brings considerable responsibility. You must have such a belief that you can do it – live the dream, and you will commit your time, your energy and your money to making it happen. You will allow nothing to stand in the way of the commitment.

Commitment means getting rid of doubt. You have to believe in your dream and believe in yourself with every fiber of your being. If you find people trying to dissuade you, I can guarantee there is a hidden agenda going on with them. You remove negative forces from your thought process. You awake each day with a positive commitment to move forward – to be in a win-win situation with your dream.

We can't preach enough that once you have your dream, set your values, determine your vision, and define your manifesto;

you must honor those traits and make the commitment to move forward. You have all the right support structure in place.

Doubt will kill commitment every time. Commitment means to remove doubt from your plan so that you are a positive force moving forward at all times.

Like the "little train who could", you can make it over any mountain with determination, guts and commitment.

When you are asked if you are going to do it….say "I am" not "I think I can". You are a person in charge of your own destiny…. you know you can! The Little Train book should have been saying "I will do it" and not "I think I can"!

Sheer will through commitment wins every time. Ironically, with strong commitment, people believe in you more. They believe anyone that is committed has to be right. You become a magnet of the right people who will help you get there because they believe in what you believe in by the power of positive thinking. It is my belief, over these last years of mentoring that most law firms FAIL because there is no follow-through. There was a mirage of excuses ranging from lack of time and the need to make money to pay the bills to lack of commitment to the plan. It didn't matter. The lawyer or the law firm owner that stayed the course and executed the plan won every time.

The "Do or Die" theory sounds radical, but you must believe in your dream and your plan that much. It must be an all or nothing attitude. Commitment and execution are like battering rams that knock down barriers and allow you to break through them.

One of the hardest lessons we learned early on was getting a commitment from the client. Because we have a passion for what we do, we tended to give away lots of free advice. We would try to accommodate the client when it was convenient to them. In other words, we thought we were doing our client a favor. Because the client had no commitment – it was free and only when convenient – they were not committed.

We became frustrated because we knew what we had to say and how we could help would be all it took. Once we said "no more" and started placing a monetary value on our services and insisting the client commit to "going for the gold", the success rate went up. In other words, we made the client commit to the dream and with an investment of time, energy and money the client wanted to succeed.

We ask our clients to tell us what the most important thing in their lives is right now. Because we are involved they always tell us turning around their lives or their firms. We then have them go through their past week with us and tell us how much time they spent on their plan and their dream. More likely than not we find very little time committed to executing the plan.

If anyone has ever seen project management software or used it, it can be your best friend or your worst enemy. One lawyer we know had us buy him the best project management software possible. We set up the schedules and objectives that had to be met each week. All the tasks assigned to the stakeholders involved in moving forward were set. As you may know, if one person fails to meet their deadline and someone else is contingent upon that completion, the line goes from green to red. Within ten days, every line on the project was red! It was because those that could make the plan work simply could not set aside ANY time to work on it.

We met as a team and decided that the growth and development of the firm was crucial to the success of this law firm owner's personal plan. He closed his firm every Friday to have work done on his plan, and he was very public in his views both with his firm and his clients.

You apply the same logic to life planning. The 'do or die' attitude is going to make an impact on what you do each day. You get up each morning knowing you are working on your plan. You put it in your planner. You take action. You meet milestones. You don't let your life plan timeline turn red because you didn't meet a commitment.

Public commitment wins every time. If you say you are going to make a million dollars, believe me you will. It is an internal clock that creates a force of energy that will allow you to succeed if nothing else through sheer will.

Commitment believes you have bought into your dream hook, line and sinker. Forward motion is the execution of the plan. One does not work without the other.

Dave's wisdom

The prime lesson my father taught me was to be true to my word. So, right away you know what one of my values is. Project Managers live and die by their word. In fact, it drives me nuts if someone says they are going to do something by a certain date and don't. I might add I am involved with a partner who is somewhat more lax in this area than I am (no comment!). However, I realized when working on a project I could commit because I saw the time line, saw things that had to be done, and could get them done.

What I didn't know how to do was commit with my heart. In other words, specifics are easy to accomplish, but when you are being asked to commit your heart, mind, and soul to a dream that you want, a dream you believe in, it starts getting dicey. I never moved forward with my success until I simply said I was going to take chances.

Through the years, I learned that not everything is an absolute. Sometimes I had to learn to state my intentions in less than absolute terms. I started acting as if I were already successful. I talked openly about my dream and what I was doing. I let so many people know I was on this road I was taking I had no choice but to go down it. Once I started committing myself 100%, I suddenly realized it was happening. With determination and commitment, you can accomplish anything. A commitment to your dream is a commitment to you.

This seems like a simple lesson to learn, but every client has experienced trouble with this concept. The problem is reality! In other words, every day struggles get in the way and steal your resources. It does not take long to discover you are no longer on the path. I would ask each client, how much time, money or energy was spent on the plan. Then look at the calendar and find all events related to the plan canceled or delayed. My only solution I have for this is to decide to do at least one thing every day to work on the plan. It could be some time or some other resource, but whatever it is, you will not cancel.

Finally, this is where my theory about trump cards comes in. There is always a trump card that gets played when you try to go down your path. Frankly my trump card is Cheryl. I want to please Cheryl and even though my plan has milestones I have to take into consideration if it affects Cheryl.

Here's what I have figured out. Know who holds the trump cards. I need to think if Cheryl really is the trump card or if it is something I am using to avoid going down the road. Maybe I am looking for the excuse. If you don't execute your plan, you don't win. If you stay the way you are, you will always be the way you are. Play those trump cards wisely.

TRUTH # 7: DON'T BE A CLIFFHANGER

We would presume everyone knows the term "cliffhanger". It is that part of the story where your heart is in your throat, and you don't know if you can turn one more page or take one more step. The author then steps way and just leaves you hanging for awhile. With a plan in place, we can guarantee you when you take the first step you are going to be in for a "cliff hanger".

Nothing won by faint heart is true in being healthy, wealthy and wise. You cannot sit on the sidelines and play it safe. Truth be told, it is boring. You have to leap off the cliff and not be a cliffhanger; stopping where it gets most exciting but scary. You have to have the desire to keep going to see what happens.

Our best guess is that 95% of all people who meet us think we are risk takers! They are right, but we are known as "calculated risk takers". While I am known to run off the cliff and learn to fly, the truth of the matter is I have a secret parachute no one is aware of.

In the beginning, I told you that my parachute was the people who surround me. They help me soar by keeping me focused, protecting my back, seeing my weaknesses, and cheering me on. I have as you do lots of other things in my parachute. I call these my character virtues.

I trust my instincts. The difference between success and failure in my opinion is your willingness to listen to your inner voice. The quicker you do it the quicker you make a decision and get where you want to go. Trust yourself!

Every day I learn something new. I am very open minded. I listen to others. I figure there are people out there who can teach me something. I have a willingness to learn and improve myself daily. Thus, I am more confident when I see how things work. Stagnation kills you.

I believe this universe is running by someone a lot smarter than me. I think I am here by design and plan, and I have a purpose. I feel it in my heart, so I keep moving forward. I think to succeed you have to have at least a belief in a higher power. I don't care what name you put on it. I think you just have to know this. This has nothing to do with religion. It has to do with purpose.

I am an accepting person. I don't think a person's color, ethnicity, sexuality, gender, religion, or political views make them unworthy to share my space. I don't tolerate people who are, and as a result my life is very rich and surrounded by amazing people who energize me to get where I am going.

I truly believe you have to be of service in this world. We have a duty to protect this beautiful word we have and help others. We don't have to do a lot, but we have to believe it. I believe in a butterfly wing movement. From here we can create a tsunami in Japan. Cause and effect.

The bottom line is that if you are a person of the world, someone who can think and believe and dream and execute and have a strong parachute you should make the leap. Add to all these your real values, your own virtues, your dream, a commitment to do it and an action plan and your landing where you want to be softer than you think.

Calculated risk takers always know they will be okay even through adversity. They know exactly how far to push the button but aren't afraid to step up to the door to ring the bell. Sitting on the sidelines will never get you beyond where you are right now. Frankly that is why you are reading this book. You have always wanted to go for the gold but have stayed on the sidelines where it is safe and protected.

If you are worried, then we suggest you tell us the worst thing you think can happen. Then accept it, prepare for it, and move on. Okay, so maybe the IRS is a different matter, but generally there is nothing worse than death. In my mind, nothing is worse than a boring death. You are positive and believe in yourself, or you are finished before you start.

Let's examine some things we have heard from others:

"I have responsibilities to my family". This means that I am worried I will fail and if so my family will see me a failure. Well frankly if you want to be responsible show your family what it means to live a dream, have a passion for what you do, and become successful. Have you ever heard someone say of his or her father, "Boy, my old man played it safe"? Nope! They say, "My old man could make it happen". "I am too old". Hogwash! I won't bore you with all the countless people over the age of 60 or 70 who have made millions, or have changed careers and made a difference with this world. What this really means is that you are trying to convince yourself that you won't make the grade and age is it. Age has nothing to do with dreams. For God sake's think of it this way – do you want to go out living, laughing and loving life at its fullest or do you want to sit on the front porch and watch the world go by?

"I will lose everything I own". Will you really? Don't make general statements that may or may not be true! Do you know how many millionaires there are today who have lost everything they own, some more than once? Admittedly I would think once would be enough before you got smart and had a better plan. Reread the chapter on making a pwan!

For those of you who have promised your children a college education the truth of the matter is they will be better people if they do it themselves. Trust me they will live their dream a lot quicker than you will. Your goal should be to make as much money as you need to live your dreams, then spend all of it, and leave only enough to buy this book and give it to your children.

We recently met a man who in his prior life was a 51 year old lawyer with a successful practice. He always felt there had to be more than life. He told us that one night he simply went home and told his wife that he was not going to practice law and he was willing to live in a tent with a lantern if he had to, but he had to do something else or die. His wife didn't leave him. His children still loved him. He had an idea and a plan. He went on to be a successful contractor and businessperson, making more than he ever dreamed he could make and enjoying life. Simply put he figured out what was the worst that could happen, accepted it and then made the leap of faith.

To take a calculated risk, first you have to understand the risk. I had a client one time who wanted to open up a restaurant (God help us!). His plan was well thought out except his business plan was to go ask money from banks who understand that 80% of all restaurants the first year fail. He failed to take into account that (1) his business plan made no provision for a salary for himself (can't figure out how he expected to feed his family of four); (2) it didn't plan for failure (he assumed hundreds would flock to his restaurant daily), and (3) he wasn't willing to put up any collateral. I needn't tell you what the bank's answer was when he asked for a capital infusion. The only thing going for him was the fact he could make the best ribs in the world.

I made him step back and become more realistic about what he wanted to do. His dream was to make lots of money selling lots of ribs and barbeque. Trust me in North Carolina this has great potential as a good idea as I believe more ribs and barbeque are eaten in North Carolina than anywhere else.

The first thing we did was figure out what it would take for him and his family to survive for two years. This was what it would take to allow him to commit to his dream. We then analyzed what his strengths and weaknesses were. Well his strength was he really did make the best ribs and barbeque I have ever eaten. His weakness was he didn't know how to run a business.

We then decided that he needed (1) a good mentor for business teachings (2) a good lawyer (3) a good CPA and (4) a friendly lender who helped people realize dreams. The lawyer, CPA, and I did a forecasting based upon a conservative approach to building the business. We factored in a salary for him. We created put a marketing plan. We created a business plan. We factored in our costs. We minimized as much risk as possible. He took his assets and put them on the line. He found an entrepreneurial lender who was willing to invest in the business as long as he had a good business team around him. In other words, we put as much into play that would help him succeed. In his mind and ours, he had done all he could do to take a very good calculated risk.

Someone asked me what it took to get beyond a cliff-hanger. That is easy: A good value system, a strong team of people who believe in you and your plan, a well documented road-map, people who believe in you, and a strong heart and commitment. All else is fluff.   .

Dave's wisdom

I am Mr. Average. I don't create waves; I don't rock the boat, and I definitely don't jump off the cliff. I analyze, manage, and recheck everything to make sure nothing goes wrong. I anticipate, plan, and hedge my bet as best I can. Heck I won't even go up to the cliff's edge in case the cliff starts to crumble. Be glad to look at it from a safe distance to develop my plan.

After I started dreaming and accumulating thoughts of the future, I decided that some risk had to be in the plan. Simply put I got tired of being Mr. Average. I realized cliff jumpers were getting all the good stuff. It looked as if like they were having fun as they stood up in boats rocking back and forth. I saw that even in the agony of defeat there was the thrill of the chase. I wanted to feel that sensation when I got up and went throughout the day. My thinking still included packing a parachute.

I admit quite candidly that the first time I ran to the edge of the cliff and looked down I felt a sharp kick in my posterior (it could have been Cheryl, tired of my not making the leap). Then I figured what the heck, the others were leaping and flapping their wings, and they were flying, and I leaped. I still get that clutch in my stomach and the lump in my throat, but I also have exceeded all my expectations. I think success is the ability to sit on a porch when you are 90 years old and NOT saying "what if".

The truth of the matter is that there is a secret to all this. Of course you have to have a well thought out plan, but you need something more. You need a true friend that has your best interest. Someone that will tell you – gosh that is a stupid idea, or someone that will catch you if you fall off that cliff. That became my parachute. It is your option to say thanks and jump anyway. I learned early on that no man is an island. My interpretation of that is it can get very lonely when you are falling and when you succeed it is great to have someone to tell.

TRUTH # 8: BE BEST IN SHOW

Please tell me that you can't pass up the Westminster Kennel Show. Each year I swear to God I am not going to watch a bunch of dogs prance around an arena particularly when they tell me how much they cost. However each year I get hooked to see who is best in show. Note the words "Best in Show" not best in breed.

What absolutely amazes me is that sometimes it is the ugliest dog in the whole event. However they exhibit confidence and there is that something special that sets the dog apart from all others. You may be the smartest, the brightest, the wealthiest, or even the best looking person there ever has been, but that doesn't make you best in show.

The question is: what is the extra quality you need to have others don't? Certainly, you should always strive to be the best you can be at what you do. It may not be everyone's cup of tea, but it is your cup. People are drawn to people who try to be the very best they can be. It matters not what your dream is, how rich you become, or how successful others see you. It is what you believe you have become.

By being the best you can be, you are more confident. You are as secure in yourself that you can and will achieve what is best for you that will make you rise above others. The next time you are at a large event look around at who are the peacocks and who are the eagles. Eagles soar higher, and they are confident in themselves. They don't have to prove a thing; peacocks do.

The extra quality that is needed is the gift of character virtues that make you the best in show. These virtues define the moral fiber that runs through you. It is what everyone else sees as you ask them to take a stake in your success.

You and your dream simply will not succeed without what I call moral fiber or character. I believe every person has it within them to lead a good and productive life, sometimes surviving childhood and environment that would cause others to fail. Somewhere during this time of testing, your character becomes tested, and you develop good character virtues. You may learn kindness because you suffered unkindness. Virtues are developed, honed, and maintained. We learn and hold our virtues close because of the life and people we are exposed to. Good people make us better. Bad people should be avoided. It's such a simple thing.

People with strong character fiber don't fall apart when the going gets tough. They are sought out by others simply because they are persons of character. You can't teach it. You can't give it to you. You have to own it.

Being best of show truly means you know you are a person of character, and you don't need to prove it. People follow you by choice. They are secure in the knowledge you know where you are going and how to get there. Don't be intimidated by perceived success demonstrated by others. You don't want to be a peacock – you want to be an eagle. Stay true to your dreams and your beliefs. Follow your plan. Take the risk. Be your best.

Whatever your dream, whatever your plan, whatever the risk you should always do it with a determination to be Best in Show.

Dave's wisdom

We are living in an amazing time. The world is moving faster than we can keep up. A year ago I refused an I-phone. Today I run my business with one.   I am being exposed on a daily basis to many things good and bad. This world is big, and it is small. It all depends on your perspective.

Over the many years with Catalyst, I have been focused on theory: business management, self-mastery, leadership and strategic planning. I merged those skills with all my experiences and worked with Cheryl to create a new focus called "Living an Unbalanced Life with Joy". All of the principles I learned seemed to mess together for this new focus. My first reaction to this new material was – gosh this is common sense. After teaching it for a year, this concept is not easy for many to grasp.

We are created through learning and growth and development of skills that are in all of us. Sometimes we slowly develop our skills as we grow and learn. Just as often there may be a set of circumstances that forces us to learn the art of character development to allow ourselves to realize a vision we have for ourselves and our careers. The bottom line, we are what we make our self.

People of character are people positive. They are always looking to find the best in people and help others walk the path to success. They encourage and motivate you to want to do things and do it right. They are not negative people. They generate excitement in others. They create leaders. They can motivate others. They are organized. They plan. They take all these skills to reach the vision they have. All of these traits can be learned.

Unfortunately, there are also negative people that convince themselves that the world is cold, they cannot do something, or that people are bad. They live in fear. I see people so frustrated or fearful that they are frustrated, mad or in tears. When I point out that they are the reason for this state of mind, they get defensive. It is hard to get them out of this state of fear.

TRUTH #9: THERE IS ALWAYS A BOTTOM LINE

The final trick to being successful is being accountable for what you do, what you say, and how you bring the dream to its fruition. You can't just be going off in different directions. A good plan has certain benchmarks or goals that must be met. Being responsible for what has to be done means you know the seriousness of accountability.

Being accountable means being answerable, beholden, responsible and obliged. Thus, you are answerable to yourself and others who believe in you. You are beholden to those that make the journey with you. You are responsible to yourself and responsible for others to do the very best you can do and deliver the product you promised. You are obliged to complete the journey.

Accountability is what brings the dream together. Accountability becomes more important when you ask others to join in to make the dream happen. The pressure to succeed is accountability to your dream. I think what makes most people succeed is they feel a personal sense of accountability to win, to succeed, and to go beyond the wildest of hopes.

Accountability for all that you do and all that you say will be delivered if you do not deviate from your values, your vision, your mission or your plan. You absolutely cannot leap off the cliff unless you are willing to bear the burden of accountability.

Here is the tricky part – failure is not failure to be accountable. I have seen many people fail, but they tried their best, and they held themselves accountable even for their failures. It is when you deny your part in the success or failure of a dream that you are doomed from the start.

At all times in your journey you must be responsible for your actions and willing to accept the consequence of the actions. I will take a person who fails but understands the accountability for failure over a success who isn't willing to be held accountable. The latter will never make it long term. Mistakes will happen – that is why there are erasers on the ends of pencils.

A willingness to be held accountable indicates the strength of character that cannot be taught. You want to build a dream that withstands the test of time. Accountability in all phases of your journey will get you there. The people you take along on this journey must also be willing to be accountable and responsible for their actions in allowing you to succeed.

When all else is said and done, you and you alone are accountable for your success. No one made you dream the dream or live the dream. I have a belief that accountability is what makes you succeed even when you fail. It is a mark of character to hold yourself accountable for what you do and what you say and thus I would caution you to be willing to be held to the standard of accountability.

Dave's wisdom:

Being accountable is the first step in solving the problem. If everything that happens to you is due to the actions of someone else, why would you ever feel compelled to put any energy of your own to fix it? First of all, you never see a problem. Second, if you did it, is not your fault anyway. You will not build any self-esteem or self confidence. You are basically stalled with no growth and no progress along your path. I have met people that are terrified to admit they were wrong. They build the greatest stories while trying to rationalize what happened.

People of character take responsibility for themselves. If you want to find joy, take responsibility for your actions. Believe in yourself, and invest time and energy in honing the skills of character. You cannot fix anything that you are not responsible for, so own it. Start simple; no sense beating yourself up too much the first time. The next time you say something that turns out to be wrong, just admit you were wrong. The first time will hurt, but you get used to it. The best manager I ever met at IBM stopped a project and admitted that he was wrong long before it escalated into a major issue. He protected his team, came up with a plan to recover and ultimately saved the company lots of money.

I have seen people spend so much of their resources proving that they were right that they had none left to walk their path. Not only did it drain their resources but nobody outside of themselves cared. Everyone else was focused on being right. Kind of a no win situation. Get back on your path and start working on your vision. Recognize that there may be more than one right answer. Focus on spending resources to realize your dream.

TRUTH # 10: LIFE IS NOT PERFECT BUT IT CAN BE JOYFUL

If I could teach anyone anything, it would be this one fact. Life is not perfect. It is never going to be perfect. No one person is perfect. They never will be. Yet life can be lived with a great deal of joy with lots of imperfect living and people.

As I enter the winter of my life (well I think it is Summer, but I will bow to the experts) I find myself thinking about this life I have had and what made the difference. Why is my life one of joy now? Why do I find myself feeling content and at peace? What makes me wake up each day with excitement? What causes me to understand true empathy? What makes me recognize the way I live my life is the purpose I am meant to accomplish? Somewhere along this journey I have been on to something that made the click for me. I just wished I had learned it earlier.

I have searched and read and searched again to try to help others see the difference between being joyful and being happy. Thus, this I believe.

Happiness is fleeting. It is driven by toys we can buy or things we can accomplish that show others what we did. It is a momentary thing that allows you to smile and feel good about yourself and life. If you go buy your red convertible, that is happiness. You feel great. You look good. Been there. Done that. At some point, the car needed washing, the payments were due, it becomes winter time, the top whistled, and my happiness was gone. It was a short quick fix that made me smile.

You may have earned your MBA and you were happy when you saw how proud everyone was. While you did it for yourself, you have made yourself happy because it impacted other people. That moment on the stage gives way to the daily grind of working to support a family, and the shine of the MBA is simply the initials at the end of your name.

Joy is much more inside you. It is that part of you that feels the pulse of life. It allows you to feel in harmony with the world as a whole. It is the peace of your spirit that comes with seeing beyond the physical senses we have. It is knowing that we have a place in this world and that our character and our purpose is understanding this. Joy is feeling right about yourself.

My joy is increased when I find myself feeling more and more right about who and what I am within my place in this world. It is the rightness of this universe that becomes a part of you.

That is when you really have peace and contentment.

For all of you who say I must have left my reality genes a chapter ago, let me tell you this. I have tried it both ways. I have made myself very happy. I have made myself very joyful. Of all the things I did to make me happy, the only thing that makes me feel right about myself is inside me.

Joy is not to be messed with. I have a favorite saying; i.e. 'don't you dare step on my joy'. It is an integral part of me, and when you mess with my joy you mess with my breathing. I am starting to understand that the soul is where you feel the joy. In the end, the state of your soul is what matters isn't it.

Dave's wisdom:

After all these years, I have boiled down this theory of life into a few simple elements. There must be a set of truths and principles that you believe in. They should be greater than yourself so you can fall back on them. With that belief and resulting values, you must have a purpose for your life, a dream that provides focus for your life, and a vision that you can develop a passion for.

That is just the stake in the ground or the starting point. You have to have a plan to realize your dream and actually execute that plan. There is a great benefit to being positive and accountable for your life. Catch yourself when you feel frustrated, depressed of just plain mad and ask if you are on the right path. How did you cause this negative emotion? What interpretation did you provide that may have caused you to react the way you did. Now gradually climb out of that pit and get back on your path.

THE FINAL THOUGHT

People who live their dreams and follow the rocky road of uncertainty to success are doing it the way they must do it. Never take the easy way and the safe way because you will be in the same place today as you were yesterday.

People who have gone for the gold tend not to walk a straight path. Their road is one filled with rocks and pebbles and occasional boulders. It will be the one avoided because it is not a comfortable one to travel. The perseverance to stay on track on the under-used road less traveled will make you a success because it is the one to success.

I will also tell you it is the most fun road to take. Each day begins with a new adventure and you will have to make decisions which fork to take. It will have surprises (I call these surprises wuck-a-lars; those things that hide along the side of the road and reach out and grab you if you aren't careful). It will have rewards around a curve when you least expect it. This book got into my head right after I was told I had a rare form of cancer, stage IV. During the time of treatment, I was told again and again that it was my attitude that was making the difference. Trust me, surgery and twelve weeks of radiation/chemo doth an attitude make. Remarkably, during the darkest hours I kept thinking how blessed I have been with my life. When I realized that I had some odds going against me, I took stock of my life (everyone who gets cancer does this), and I realized that in the long run what was going to make the difference was my belief system about living life. I realized that all my life I taught others how to live, and if I was going on a path of no return then I could be the role model on how to live this life.

Out of all of this came a desire to let others know what life is really about, how to become all you can be, and how to be able to have it all whatever that might be for each person. More importantly, to give people hope that they are indeed champions of life and deserve a Gold Medal for living life to the fullest.

We Americans love instant gratification, and perhaps we have forgotten too many of life's lessons from previous generations. We are in a time in our lives where there is hope and despair. Our world is filled with perilous times and perilous events, but always there is a way to make it better if we are just willing to do it. We can either be doomsday-sayers or dream-makers. If you read this book carefully, you will realize that there are ways to have anchors in storms that propel you forward. The trick is to have constant forward motion at all times.

I am not wealthy. I am not highly educated. I am not the best Mom in the world. I sometimes forget to be a good friend, and I believe I could do better as an Aunt. The world deserves more from me than I am giving it right now.

Notwithstanding this, I believe my life is successful, and that takes into consideration all the bad storms I have weathered. It includes things I wish I hadn't done, and things I wish I had and may never do. The reason I believe I am successful is because I am not sure I have quite finished achieving all the success I want. Each time I think I am where I could say I have achieved success I get another scathingly brilliant idea and off I go again. Thus, I believe my life has been made up of different successful events and then I ask why I have been so fortunate to have enjoyed the success I have had.

I am successful because I have people in my life who allow me to dream, who make me walk the walk and talk the talk and wouldn't accept less than success from me. These people had believed in me when even I didn't believe. I have been kicked, prodded, and thrown down the path of success by those who wouldn't take "no" for an answer.

I have realized that I have indeed found the gold, and the gold is that feeling of contentment I get at the end of another day when I sit on my back porch and realize I'm at peace.

Dave's Wisdom and Final Thoughts:

Early in life I wondered if anything happens for a purpose. Is there really a master plan for this life? I came to believe not only that there is a plan, but I was part of it. When Cheryl and I met I was recovering from surgery after Prostate Cancer. I was in deep depression about everything that happened and took a chance one winter day to meet Cheryl. Since then we have managed to help each other through life's little challenges. Somehow we never had major events at the same time and always were there for the other. There were so many other things that happened that reinforced my feeling that there was a purpose for all this. I became very interested in how this life worked. I read every book I could find on living the good life, self-mastery and soon realized that I already had both. Actually I began to notice that all the books said the same thing.

Life's path is going to have peaks and valleys. It is going to embrace you, and it will kick you in the teeth occasionally. Your job, should you decide to accept it, is to live life. Discover your passion and get out there on the path.

So perhaps there is a final truth. That truth is that in the end, what matters are the people you surround yourself with and stay the course with you. This can be family, friends, or business acquaintances, but they all have one thing in common; a desire that you succeed at whatever your heart's dreams are. When you find people like this, you keep them close. In the end, they are the key to finding the pot of gold.

From Both of us

Don't ever settle for mundane. Don't put up with mediocrity. Put passion in your life, do the unthinkable, break it if it is not broken, embrace change, and welcome risk. Get up each morning eager to see what can be thrown at you. Step up to the plate. Learn to live a joyful unbalanced life on purpose. The alternative is simply unthinkable.

Both of us truly wish for you to find your heart's dream. It is that part of what we love to do - help people find their dreams. We can't be there for everyone, and thus the book is written.

So go out there, live your dream, and if it gets a bit shaky, email us and we will try to shore you up. Use those instincts of yours that are usually right. Know that when all is said and done, it is how you take your journey that counts, not the destination.

OUR MANIFESTO

CHERYL LEONE AND DAVE FAVOR

JOY AND ENTHUSIASM

We place a high value on being in a state of joy* and enthusiasm. We will seek to find humor and wisdom in events knowing that to do less is not who we are. We will strive daily to find joy in that which we encounter, and we will start our day with enthusiasm and excitement for who we are and what we have in our life.

Joy: A state of emotion evoked by well-being, success, or good fortune or by the prospect of possessing what one desires.

PARTNER RELATIONSHIP

We value our committed relationship without reservation. We recognize we are fully accountable for this relationship and we each will be a worthy partner. We accept the risk of vulnerability and accept each other. We work towards allowing both of us to move forward in a manner that meets our needs, individually and together. We value the friendship that we have. We accept the gift of being valued. We will not allow others to do anything that would destroy our integrity as a committed couple.

We have a **passion to support each other** with respect for each other's needs, talents and self worth. To establish an environment of trust we must provide respect and passion. Part of our belief system would refer to this as my responsibility to the collective consciousness, and to our relationship.

CONTINUOUS LEARNING AND IMPROVEMENT

We seek continuous knowledge and understanding of all things with the goal of improving our lives. We will maintain an open mind and be willing to have challenged our thoughts and our beliefs so that we may have a greater understanding of those things that we need to sustain us. We seek to share our knowledge and will expect others to share knowledge with us as it is through shared knowledge that we grow and gain wisdom.

SPIRITUALITY

We believe in a higher power. We believe that there is some intelligent design for this universe that we are in, and we believe that we are part of that design. We believe that we have a purpose and that we are not isolated. We further believe that we have freedom of choice and that we can discover our purpose and move forward. To discover our purpose we must maintain an open mind with a sincere desire to have our faith strengthened through knowledge, experience, and the values of others.

Using that process, we believe that our purpose is to share what we have learned, look for opportunities to contribute, and develop supportive relationships. We further believe that our mandate is to have compassion for and understanding of others and to be of service without an expectation of reward or recognition. We believe to do less is to reject a gift that we have been given. We will walk a daily path with that as our goal.

We will keep constant in our thoughts that what we do affects not only us but others. We believe we are a part of a total collective human community with an obligation to affect change through thoughts and actions. We will ensure that we will not intentionally cause harm to others. We recognize that it is not our role to judge others in their actions or beliefs but to live our life with a commitment to our beliefs. We will approach the end of this life, not with fear, but with understanding that this is a transition of this life and who and what we are will be our legacy.

FAMILY

We believe that a family sustains its members; that it supports and nourishes the members through the span of the family. We will strive to build a strong extended family that creates a safe, positive and supportive place for all members to thrive. We promote the family to have a feeling of being loved, belonging to a group, and being nurtured by it. Though seeking closeness with the members, we believe there is a balance between being together and being separate. We promote and encourage family members to develop their own individuality while being supported and confident within the family. This supportive environment is a two way street. We believe in being supportive instead of enabling. We expect support in return. We believe that interaction between family members is not an act of obligation but one created out of love and respect for each other.

We will be worthy of the trust they have in us, and be an anchor for them when they need it. We will remember that we are a role model as to how one lives life with purpose.

SELF

We will value ourselves as an individual; wisely using our time, energy and intellect to support our own needs. We will respect ourselves for exactly who we are, recognizing that we do not need to be what others imagine us to be. We will make sure that we keep a balance in our health and well-being and take care of ourselves because it is only when we take care of ourselves we can care for others.

OUR MANIFESTO

Our life's mission is to educate, support and empower ourselves and others who are committed to creating and consistently living a life of more awareness, joy, passion and purpose and to be and become active participants in the creation of a more conscious, service oriented, joyous and loving world. To this end our goal is to be of service to others. Our legacy in this life is that when all is said and done we made a difference; with each other, our family, our friends and this world. For us, it is not necessary to have reward or recognition, but because it has been the right way to treat this gift of life we have.

www.ingramcontent.com/pod-product-compliance
Lightning Source LLC
Chambersburg PA
CBHW071812170526
45167CB00003B/1283